Beginners Guide to Web Designing
With Google™ Sites

Enhanced Version

TARIKU TESSEMA

DEDICATION

Para mi familia

TABLE OF CONTENTS

Chapter One Where Do I Start?   1

Chapter Two Technical Jargon   9

Chapter Three Signing up for Google Sites   17

Chapter Four Creating Web Pages   25

Chapter Five Text and Images   31

Chapter Six Videos and Calendars   39

Chapter Seven Working With Forms   49

Chapter Eight Customizing Your Site   61

ACKNOWLEDGMENTS

I would like to thank my wife Daniela for her support during this experiment and all the students who attended my Introduction to Web Design class.

New enhanced version

The new enhanced version of the Beginners Guide to Google Sites features case studies at the end of each Chapter. The case studies outline how Jane Doe,[1] a photographer, used Google Sites to create a portfolio website.

You can review Jane's portfolio website made using Google Sites and mostly freely available resources at www.photosbyjanedoe.com.

---

[1] For curious souls, Jane Doe is a fictitious photographer. Any resemblance to a real person, living or dead, is purely coincidental.

Chapter One

Where Do I Start?

One of the questions that people often ask me in my "Learn How to Design a Website in Eight Hours" class is "where do I start?" Most people, at one point or another, have seriously thought about building a website, but the idea never materialized for various reasons. The common excuses I hear include "it's too complicated," "I am still thinking about the design – should it have a (you fill in the blank) color/design?" or "I don't want to buy software – this is just a hobby thing for me." If you notice all the excuses use the same pattern of the "wait and something might magically happen" approach.

> As experience has taught me, nothing in life worth doing comes "magically" for most of us, well, unless you are Isaac Newton and you happen to take an afternoon nap right under an apple tree.

Web designing is not complicated; color is not that important and you don't need to buy software if you want to build a website.

You would have to use all the resources at your disposal if you really wanted to make a dent on your desire to do anything in life, and that applies to web design as well. So in short – it's not complicated. Color is not that important, and you don't need to buy software if you want to build a website. In just about eight hours, you can build a website and share your hobby, craft, or professional portfolio with the world.

The starting point for website development project is creating an outline of things you want to include on your website. Think of your website as a grocery store shopping cart – not the bulky one you push – but the little carriage that you wish you hadn't picked up at the store front after adding a carton of Tropicana® orange juice. Now imagine yourself walking in the digital aisles of the internet with your grocery hand basket and picking up things that you'd like to include in your website. Before adding anything shiny into your basket, you first must think about your audience. I'm going to let you in on a little secret – the website audience is everyone else in the world but you! Think of your website as a window rather than a mirror.

The website audience is everyone else in the world but you!

You should strive to have a website that anyone from any corner of the world can take a look at few pages on your site and understand your website content. If you are still struggling with website ideas, Google is your best friend. Google-search anything that comes to mind. Go ahead—try it. I'll wait. Now look at the first few websites on the search results page—did you successfully find enough information about your search word or phrase?

If you repeat the Google-search exercise a number of times and you get to a point where the sites in the search results don't have sufficient information– you just struck gold.

What does that mean? It means here is an opportunity. If you know a great deal about the thing you looked for and you have things you want to say about the topic, you are ready for a website outline.

A website outline is a written contract to hold you accountable to yourself during the website building project. It also helps you identify key aspects of your project.

Beginners Guide to Web Designing With Google™ Sites

Here is an example of a website outline:

Website Outline

In addition to keeping
you accountable, a
website outline also
helps you identify key
aspects of your
project.

Website Name:	
Website Audience:	
Website Pages:	Page 1: Page 2: Page 3: Page 4: Page 5:
Must have features (e.g. photos, events calendar, etc...):	
Nice to haves:	
Assumptions:	
Milestones:	Milestone One: Milestone Two: Milestone Three:
Launch Date:	

Example of website outline

You don't have to come up with the domain name for your site at this point, but you do need to write down a few keywords about your website in your outline.

A description of your website audience is also something you want to finalize at this point. Describe your audience in terms of age, location, interest, and any describable attributes. To keep things simple, I recommend having only five pages for your first website-building experience.

The next step in completing your website outline is to write down at least five pages you would like to have on your website. Here is a list of pages in case you need some inspiration:

Description Pages:

- About (Us)
- Person Name
- For (your audience) (e.g. For parents, For Kids)
- By work role (e.g. Staff)
- By topic (e.g. Entertainment, Art, Mission)

Contact Pages:

- Contact (Us)
- Contacts
- Location (e.g. Store)

Core Pages:

- Portfolio
- Services
- How to (fill in the blank)
- Learn
- Protect
- Membership
- Events

Supporting Pages:

- FAQ (Frequently asked Questions)
- (Any Action) Now (e.g. Buy Now, Sign Up Now)
- Sponsors

Common Website Pages

About (Us)
Person Name
For (your audience)
(e.g. For parents, For Kids)
By work role (e.g. Staff)
By topic (e.g. Entertainment, Art, Mission)
Contact (Us)
Contacts
Location (e.g. Store)
Portfolio
Services
How to _
Learn
Protect
Membership
Events
FAQ (Frequently asked Questions)
Now (e.g. Buy Now, Sign Up Now)
Sponsors
Partners
Podcasts

- Partners
- Podcasts

After you fill out the five pages you would like to have on your website, then go ahead and fill out the "must haves.". These are items that are vital to your website project. If your reason for creating a website is to sell your paintings, you might have challenges attracting visitors if you don't have photos to display your paintings. In this case, having photos would be listed as a "must have" for your site. Another example would be if your website involves sharing tips and tricks about your trade, say, how to crochet a Christmas apron to give to your lovely son-in-law. Regardless of what it is, you want to have all the details about your trade written down on actual paper before you start the process of building your website. In the crochet case – you will list "tips and tricks" as a "must have" for your site.

The next item on your website outline is "nice to haves." These are things you could get by without if you launch your website without them. For example, launching a website without a "FAQ" section or an events calendar isn't a big deal for most websites. Videos of your cat playing the piano could also wait until your website is up and running, unless your website's core message caters to feline pianists.

"Nice to haves" are things you could get by without if you launch your website without them.

Assumptions are important components on your website outline.

The only way to dispel assumptions and make sure that they will not sneak up on you when least expected is to actually put them on a piece of paper.

If your website needs photos to launch – in other words if "photos" are in your "must have" category – and you don't have photos in digital format, then your assumptions are that you have a digital camera and you can successfully take and transfer photos onto your computer. If you are launching your website to sell goods, your assumptions are that you have goods to sell in your inventory when you launch your website.

The other important items you want to jot down on your website outline are milestones. For a small website project, having three minor milestones helps you break the project into three small phases.

The first milestone can be investigating assumptions. For example, you could put in a tentative date for getting all items needed for the site— text that goes onto pages, images, goods to sell, etc.— as your first milestone. The second and third milestones can be dates that you put in the website outline depending on the time you have allocated for the project.

The last piece of information for the website outline is to put in a tentative launch date for your site. If you are building a website for the very first time, I recommend scheduling at least four weeks to work on the project before you launch the site.

You then sign the website outline to make things official. If you made it to this point – congratulations! By signing your website outline, you now have a moral contract punishable by regret anytime you touch something that is connected to an electronic source – from a toaster-oven to an iPhone - for the rest of your life. Want to avoid banishment from the digital world? Keep reading – in the next Chapter, we will work on giving you the tools that you need to build a website.

Case Study – One

Jane's Website Outline

In the course of the next eight Chapters, we will explore the topics to build a website using Google Sites. The case studies outline the journey of a photographer, Jane Doe, in creating a portfolio website using Google Sites. The first step of the process in the website design project is to fill out the website outline to flush out the project details.

Jane filled out the website outline as follows:

Website Name:	*Photos by Jane*
Website Audience:	*Businesses, entrepreneurs, families who are thinking about having a wedding ceremony*
Website Pages:	Page 1: *About Jane* Page 2: *Projects* Page 3: *Jane's Photo shoot calendar* Page 4: *Resources* Page 5: *Contact Jane*
Must have features (e.g. photos, events calendar, etc...):	• *Calendar for photo shoot availability* • *Gallery of images* • *Way to contact Jane* • *Amazon Storefront*
Nice to have:	As a result of the wealth of information that Jane has about photographing special events, she would like to have a page on her website that will list items she recommends for people to buy for events. Ideally, the items that she recommends will be easily available for people to buy on online stores such as Amazon.com.

Assumptions:	• I have images that I can feature on my new website
Milestones:	Milestone One: *Gather all photos* Milestone Two: *Have content for all five pages listed on the outline* Milestone Three: *Launch new site*
Launch Date:	*In 8 weeks*

Jane's website outline

Chapter Two

Technical Jargon

Web development is a discipline plagued by technical jargon. New platforms/programs/ techniques are developed every day to feed the vibrant digital ecosystem. Even though talking in technical jargons allows technical folks to analyze digital challenges, it might be a bit overwhelming for people who are not familiar with web development.

> A non-technical person who overhears a bunch of web developers trading technical jargon on a casual Friday might mistake the bearded developers in wrinkled Khaki pants as a bunch of actors trying to recreate a Capital One® commercial.

As the purpose of this book is to guide you through the process of building a website – while also shielding you from jargon-welding Vikings - I am not going to throw technical jargon at you, well except for a few very important terms.

For the purpose of the book, HTML is the code that runs under the hood of any web page.

Let's start with the basic jargon first - "HTML." You don't need to know what it stands for unless you are curious.[2] For the purpose of this book, HTML is the code that runs under the hood of any web page. By design, our modern-day browsers thankfully shield us from ever seeing web pages under the hood. If you have never looked at HTML code, you are in for a treat. Go to any browser of your choice (Chrome, Internet Explorer, FireFox, Safari etc.), and right click on any web page. Then select an option that says something

---

[2] OK Curious George – it stands for Hyper Text Transfer Protocol. It is the protocol that is used to transfer files from one machine to another in a TCP/IP network (sigh).

like "View Source." Your browser will most likely open a new tab(or window) and show you all the characters that make up the web page.

Let's add some more technical jargon just so that we can get it out of the way and start the hands-on portion of the book.

HTML code is written in such a way that all the code segments are nested like a Russian doll. Consider the following example.

<html></html>

The <html> is called an opening tag, and the </html> is called a closing tag. The closing tag has "/" in it to indicate that it is the terminating string. Let's see some more examples.

<html>

   <head></head>

</html>

The code above adds the tag <head> nested in the <html> tag. I will go through the significance of the various tags shortly, but for now, let's look at a more complete HTML code for displaying the word "Test" in a web browser.

```
<html>
    <head>
            <title>Test</title>
    </head>
    <body>
            Test
    </body>
</html>
```

Example of HTML code

If you write the code above into a text editor (e.g. Notepad, Notepad++) and save the file as "test.html", you have successfully created a new webpage using HTML.

If you have attempted and were successful in displaying "Test" on your browser, great. If you have problems displaying "Test" – do not worry about it as the main purpose of this exercise is just to introduce you to HTML code structure. Google Sites makes creating a website very easy as you can

10

create a website without ever looking at HTML code.

You don't need to memorize any HTML code, but having the following common elements as a reference will greatly help you in building and customizing your site.

Code	Display	Description
`<h1>Test</h1>`	Test	Header
`<h2>Test</h2>`	Test	Header
`<h3>Test</h3>`	Test	Header
`<img src="" alt="test" />`	■	Image
`<a href="">Link</a>`	Link	Link
`<div></div>`		Text/image container
`<span></span>`		Text/image container
`<p></p>`		Paragraph

`<ol>`
`    <li>One</li>`
`    <li>Two</li>`
`</ol>`
	1.One
	2.Two
		Ordered list

`<ul>`
`    <li>One</li>`
`    <li>Two</li>`
`</ul>`
	.One
	.Two
		Unordered list

`<iframe src=""></iframe>`		Embedding a web page

Common HTML elements

You don't need to memorize any HTML code, but recognizing common elements is very helpful as you build your website project.

You don't need to memorize any HTML code, but recognizing common elements is very helpful as you work on your website project.

Case Study – Two

Jane's Amazon® aStore™

One of the items that Jane wanted to add on her site is a place for website visitors to view items that Jane recommends for events. From lessons in Chapter two, Jane has learned that certain technical components of website designing, specifically "iframes," allow a website to interact with other websites. Jane has heard that certain online service providers, such as Amazon©, allow users to create an online store and organize curated items. In addition to providing a good place to organize items, Jane also has heard that she can generate affiliate marketing income using such services.

Jane used the following steps to create an online store in Amazon© aStore™that she later plans to somehow add to her Google Site.

How Jane created an Amazon® Online Store using the following steps

1. Jane went to Amazon© aStore™ website (http://astore.amazon.com/) and signed up for a new Amazon© aStore™ account.

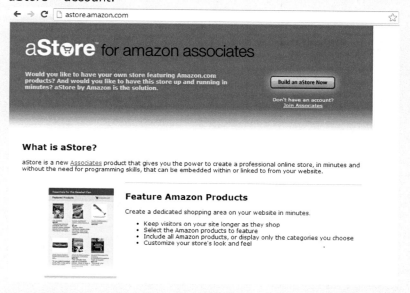

Figure 1 Amazon© aStore™

2. Jane clicked on the "Add an aStore" button after signing up for an aStore™ account.

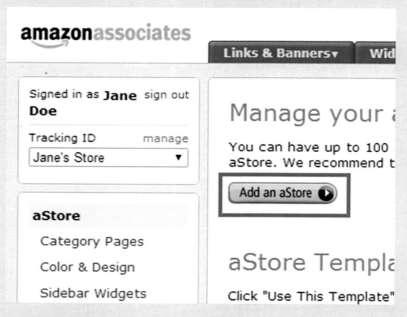

Figure 2 Adding an Amazon© aStore™

3. Jane clicked on "Add Category Page" and added a "Party Supplies" category.

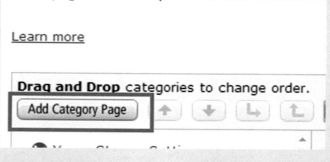

Figure 3 Adding Category Page

4. Jane added products to her newly created category page.

Jane finished up creating her Amazon store using the steps above, and in the next Chapters, she hopes to learn how she can integrate the newly created Amazon store website into her Google Sites website.

I am sure Jane would mind, but there are no penalties if you have the urge to "peek and cut" the case study lineup. You can see how the store is integrated with Google Sites in Chapter eight.

Chapter Three

Signing Up for Google Sites

The manual that was used to document all the screens and algorithms used in the Apollo module for the lunar mission in the '80s was only 150MB. So unless you are planning a solo lunar mission, you might not run into size limitation issues with Google Sites.

Google Sites is a platform that allows users to create a website free of charge. Despite the size restriction of 100MB per site (at the time I am writing this book), the size is enough for most small business and personal portfolio websites. After all, even the manual that was used to document all the screens and algorithms used in the Apollo module for the lunar mission in the '80s was only 150MB. So unless you are planning a solo lunar mission, you might not run into size limitation issues with Google Sites.

At this stage of your process, I am going to assume you have already gotten a website outline finalized and you've kicked procrastination to the curb thanks to a nagging obligation of building a website. You are now ready for some hands-on exercise and taking the first step to embark on your digital journey.

The first step in the hands-on process is to go ahead and sign up for Google Sites. If you already have a Google account (or Gmail account), you can simply sign up for Google Sites using the Google Sites link (sites.google.com).

If you have never had a Google or Gmail account, sorry to say, but you have been living in a cave for the past few years. I hope it is not a big disappointment if I told you that Twinkies have made a comeback (yes ... they were gone) and Chrysler is now owned by Fiat.

Okay for my cave dwellers, who don't already have a Google account, go to (www.google.com), and click on the link that says "Sign In". Then you will be presented with another link that says "Create Account". Click on the "Create Account" link, and follow instructions on the page to create your first Google account. If all goes well, you will then have a brand new Google account. Head over to Google Sites (sites.google.com), and sign up for Google Sites.

Head over to Google Sites (sites.google.com) and sign up for a Google Sites account.

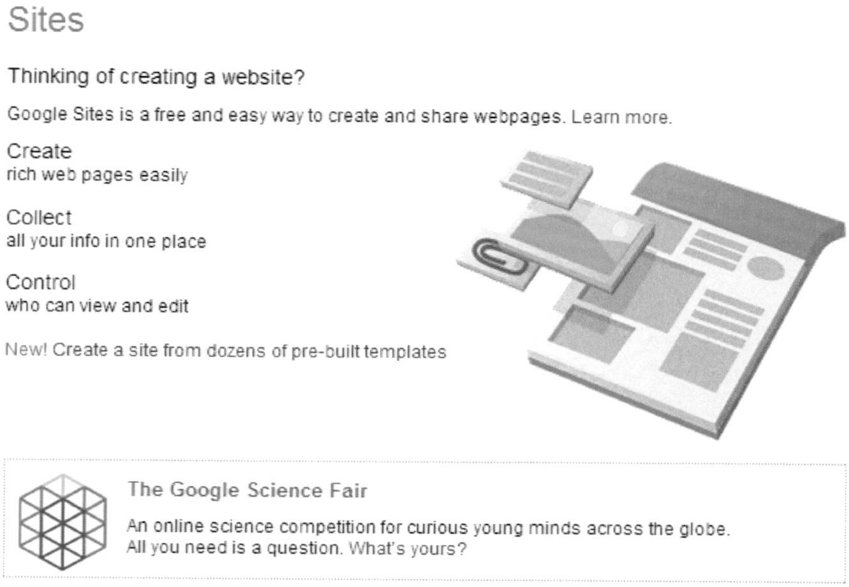

Sites

Thinking of creating a website?

Google Sites is a free and easy way to create and share webpages. Learn more.

Create
rich web pages easily

Collect
all your info in one place

Control
who can view and edit

New! Create a site from dozens of pre-built templates

The Google Science Fair
An online science competition for curious young minds across the globe. All you need is a question. What's yours?

Figure 4 - Signing up for Google Sites

If you successfully made it to the screen below, you have made it! You have now put your key in the Google Sites ignition, and your digital spaceship is now humming and ready to receive the next set of instructions from you.

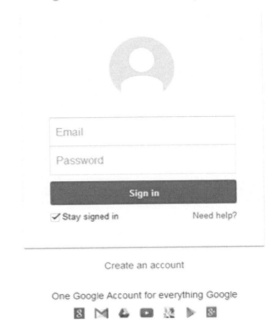

Figure 5 Google Sites after logging in

Now is a good time to revisit your website outline and go over one detail we skipped but need to finalize before you create your first site. The first thing on the list is a website name (if you don't have one listed on your website outline). My advice to you is to be flexible on your website name. As every site in Google Sites needs to be unique, you might not be able to create a website such as "LOL" (that stands for Laughing Out Loud) or "Lunar" as they are popular terms and are most likely taken. I suggest that you look at your website description and come up with a unique name that fits your needs. Your website name needs to be small and catchy. If your website name is something like "How to Make Lemonade on a Hot Summer Day," I would change that to "summer lemonade" instead for brevity.

Now with the website outline on-hand, let's go ahead and create your first website. Go to (sites.google.com), and click on the link that says "Create" on the left side of the screen. Leave everything as-is, and just type in your

I suggest that you look at your website description and come up with unique name that fits your needs.

website name on the "Name Your Site" textbox. I recommend that you use all small letters and dashes in place of spaces in your website name. So if your website name is "Summer Lemonade," change it to "summer-lemonade" instead. It is important to change spaces to dashes because it makes your website Search Engine friendly[3] and accessible to your viewers. Once you type in your site name, you will be presented with a verification code. Enter the code in the textbox, and click on "Create Link" at the top of your page.

Google Sites provides an option for users to use "pre-baked" templates that are available instead of using the plain vanilla "Blank Template." Website templates such as the "Classroom Site" or the "Soccer Team" site come with all the pages that you would need to build a new website. You can also browse additional site Themes from the Google Site gallery when creating a site by clicking on the "Browse the gallery for more" option when creating a new website.

Even though it's easy to pick one of the "pre-baked" sites when creating your first Google Site, I highly recommend not using a template for your new site. Most of the templates come with a predetermined number of web pages, and modifying or updating the site structure and look and feel might be challenging, especially if this is your first time working in Google Sites.

It is also important to note that once you pick a site template and start working on the website content, you cannot go back and switch templates for your website. If you change the site template (you will learn how to update the site settings in Chapter eight) after populating your content, all the site content you worked on will be erased, and you will lose information on your web pages.

---

[3] A single space in your website name adds three characters, namely, "%20", to the URL that users have to type in to access your site. Do yourself and everyone who visits your website a favor by not adding spaces in your website name. It might be inconvenient but true that If everyone who ever owns a website replaces spaces with dashes we might just save some energy from search engine cranking servers to spare a few trees in the Amazon.

CREATE   Cancel

Select a template to use:

Use "Blank template" for your website for now. We will explore other templates in the case study at the end of the Chapter.

Blank template

Classroom site 🔍

Soccer team 🔍

Name your site:

Site location - URLs can only use the following characters: A-Z,a-z,0-9

https://sites.google.com/site/

Figure 6 Creating a new site

If all goes well, congratulations! You now are a proud owner of a new Google site.

Case Study – Three

Jane's Test Website

Jane wanted to explore the features offered by website templates, so she took the following steps to create another new site with one of the template offered by Google Sites.

1- Jane clicked on "Create New Site" on the Google Sites account webpage.

2- Jane named her new site "janedoestest" and picked the "Soccer team" website template.

ıse:

Classroom site 🔍   Soccer team 🔍

3- Jane browsed through the pages of her new test site and continued to reading the lessons in Chapter four to learn about how to add and update new web pages in Google Sites.

Chapter Four

Creating Web Pages

The Google site you created in Chapter two already comes with a landing (home) page.[4] Before you modify your home page, let's go ahead and add some pages to your Google site.

A home page (landing page) is the first page that visitors see then they come to your website.

Scan through your website outline, and create all the pages that you have listed in your outline. Here is the set of steps for creating a new web page.

How to create a web page:

1. Go to Google Sites (sites.google.com).
2. Click on "New Page" to create a new web page.

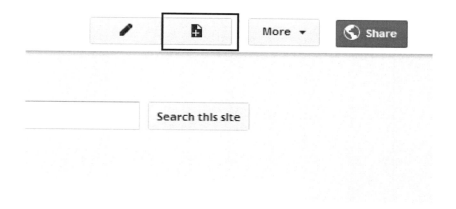

Figure 7 Creating a new page

3. Fill in the "Name your page" textbox.
   (To make your site accessible and user friendly, use all small letters and dashes in place of spaces. For example "Contact Us" would be added as "contact-us")
4. Click on "Save" to save the page

---

[4] A home page (landing) page is the first page that users see when they access your website.

Repeat the process for each page you have listed on the website outline.

Not too shabby. At this point, you already have the blue print of your site finalized. Let's get your digital house finished up by working on the content.

By default, a new Google Sites page comes with "Add Files" and "Comments" links at the bottom of the page. To make your website look polished and professional, turn off the "Add Files" and "Comments" links by using the following steps.

1- Click on "More" and then "Page Settings".

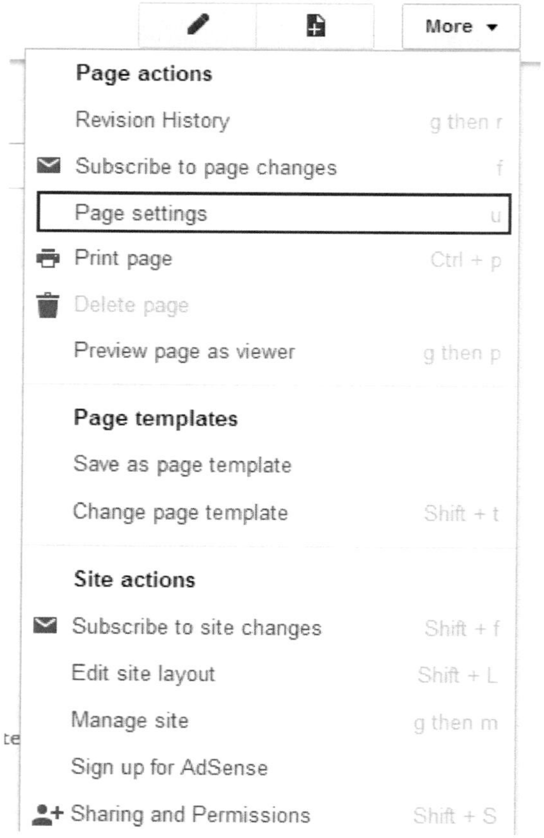

By default, a new Google Sites page comes with "Add Files" and "Comments" links at the bottom of the page.

Figure 8 Page Settings

2- Uncheck the "Allow Attachment" and "Comments" checkboxes.

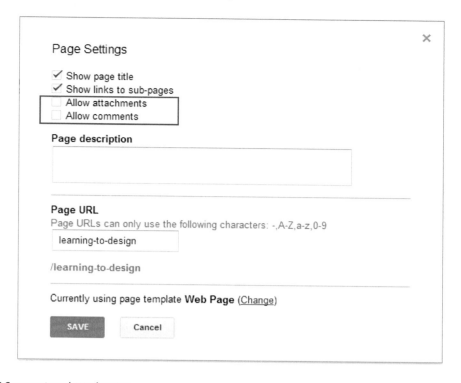

To make your website look polished and professional, turn off the "Add Files" and "Comments" options.

Figure 9 Comments and attachments

Case Study – Four

Jane's Home Page

Jane wanted to feature tile photos of the best shots that she has in her repository on the home page of her new website. Jane selected 12 of her best photos and used an image editor (Photoshop, Light box, Paint.Net) to resize each one to a size of 200 pixels by 133 pixels.

Jane then used the following steps to create a 12-image tiles home page that features the 12 photos that she has selected.

1- Jane clicked on "Edit" on the home page.

2- Jane added a 12-cell table by clicking on "Table", "Insert Table" and then selecting a 12-cell table (four columns and three rows)

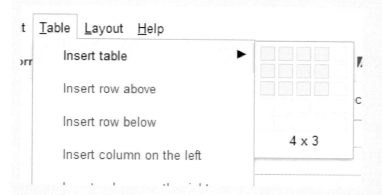

Figure 10 Adding table on a webpage

3- Jane then added an image to each cell using the following step and the following menu options.

4- Jane clicked on a cell to position the cursor in the table cell.

5- Jane then clicked on "Insert", then "Image", and clicked once on the "Upload Image" button.

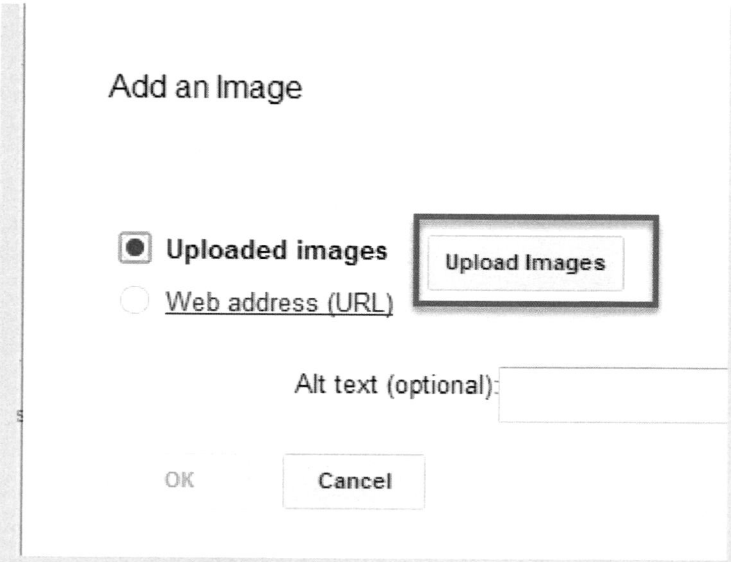

Add an Image

Uploaded images   Upload Images
Web address (URL)

Alt text (optional):

OK   Cancel

Figure 11 Uploading images

After completing Jane's case study, you might see that the home page tiles for your website might need some more refinements, such as centering them on the page and adding borders around the tiles. In the last case study of the book, we will go over the updates that Jane did to improve the overall look and feel of her website home page.

No need to scan through the remaining pages of the book to look for more information about images or spend hours crafting entries in the Google search box, like a Spreadsheet Ninja. You will learn more about images in the next Chapter (it is just a page away).

Chapter Five

Text and Images

Almost all website content can be grouped into two major categories: text and digital media (videos and images). We will get to digital media later on in this Chapter. For now, let's work on the text content of your website.

I recommend having all your content saved in your favorite text editor, such as Microsoft Word, before you start working on the text content. It's important so that you can spell check and review your website content holistically. Go through your website content with a fine-toothed comb as you would in a regular written document. After all, the contract you signed in Chapter one (your website outline) depends on it.

I recommend having all your content saved in your favorite word editor before you start working on the text for your website.

After you have reviewed your website content, you are now ready to start adding content to your website. You can add text content you have in the Microsoft® Word document into Google Sites using the following steps:

How to add text to your Google site web page:

1. Go to Google Sites (sites.google.com).
2. Click on your website name.
3. Click on the "More" drop down on the top navigation menu.
4. Click on "Manage Site".

The "More" option shows you additional options such as sharing and permissions for the webpage you have created.

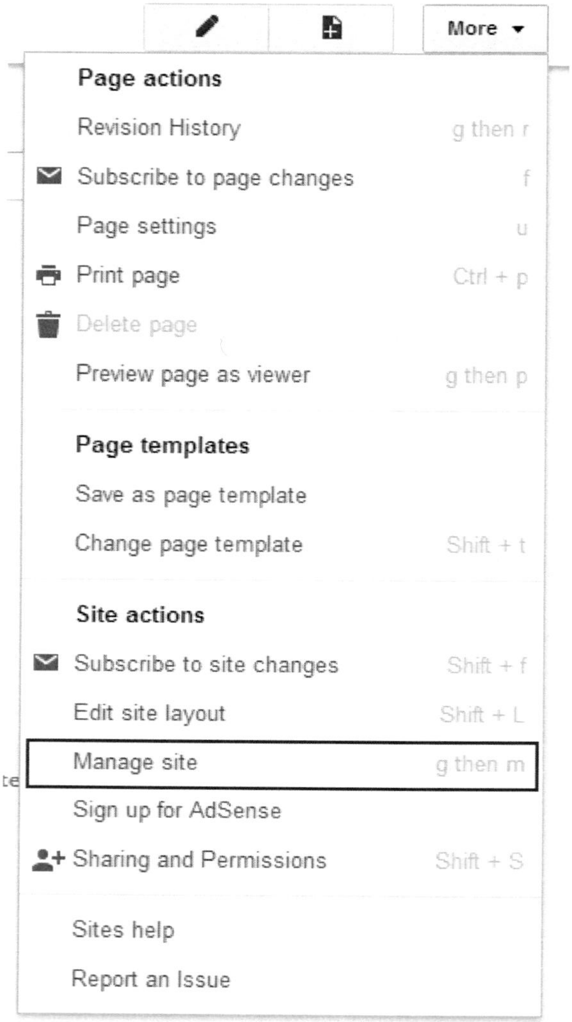

Figure 12 Site management

5. Click on "Pages" from the left navigation menu.

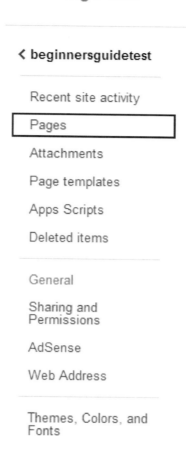

The "Pages" link under site management takes you to a page that has a list of all the web pages on your site.

Figure 13 Link to all your web pages

6. Click on the page you want to edit by clicking on the page's name.
7. Once the page loads, click on "Edit" Icon from the top menu options.
8. Copy your text from your Word Editor software, and paste the contents into the webpage text box.
9. Click on "Save" to save the page.

Repeat the process for all pages you have in your website outline. Almost there! You are now ready to start working on images for your website.

Working with Images

In our current time of imgur, Pintrest, and Tumbler, it's almost become a necessity to have images peppered in your website as website users have very short attention spans. One way to bridge the content cognition gap between avid readers and people just scanning your website is to put in a good representative image on every webpage of your website.

As the saying goes - a good image is worth a thousand clicks.

For each page you have on your website outline, find at least one descriptive image. You can always dust off your digital camera (or Smartphone) and snap a picture or two if you don't have images to go with your web content.

If you are taking your own pictures, you might want to look into photography tips. These should help you get started for now:

For each page you have on your website outline, find at least one descriptive image.

- Never take a portrait photo at mid-day (especially when the sun is out in full force).

- Never have a light source directly in front of your photo subject, and

- Never take a very low resolution photo by zooming.

If you want to just use photos taken by other people or professional images, take a close look at the copyright laws and permissions for the images before you use them on your website. Photographers and people who hold copyrights to digital artifacts are also very happy and willing to help you in your website project, provided that you ask for their permission and attribute the digital content to them in some way, shape, or form on your website.

Once you have identified the images you want to use for your site, save them on your computer or have them on a flash drive. Now to add the images into Google Sites pages, follow the steps below.

1. First log into Google Sites.
2. Click on your website name.
3. Click on "More > Manage Sites".
4. Click on "Pages".

5. Select the page you want to add your picture on by clicking on its name.

6. Click on the "Edit" icon once the page loads.

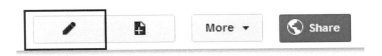

Figure 14 Editing page

7. Click on "Insert >Image"

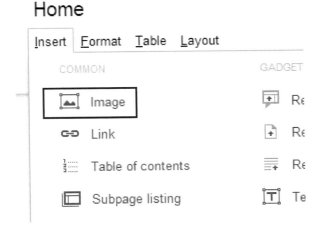

Figure 15 Inserting image

8. Click on the "Upload Image" button, and select the image from your computer or flash drive.

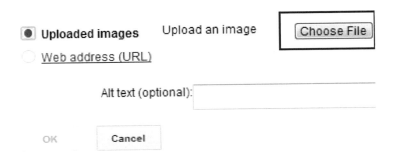

Figure 16 Upload image

9. Add a description for your image in the "Alt Text (Optional)" field.

It's important to add a description to your image as it allows users who have visual disabilities to know about the image on your web page.

10. Click on "OK" to add the image to your web page.
11. Once the image is added to your web page, you can hover over the image with your mouse to activate the image editor panel.

Figure 17 Image editor panel

Once an image is uploaded into Google Sites, it shows up every time you click on the "Insert >Image" option so that it is easier for you to add it to web pages.

The "S" menu makes your image smaller, the "M" menu option makes your image medium size, and likewise, the "L" menu option makes your image larger. If you want the original image size, you can click on "Original" in the image editor panel.

Repeat the process for each image you want to add to your page. I recommend having one image on top of your content and having another image in the middle of your content to fully engage your visual audience.

Case Study – Five

Jane's Website Pages

After creating the home page in the previous Chapter, Jane wanted to continue creating all the pages she has in her website outline from Chapter one. Jane used the following steps to create the pages in a two-column layout format.

1- Jane clicked on the "New Page" icon.

Figure 18 Create new page icon

2- As Jane was working on the "About Jane" page, she put in "about" as the page name and clicked on the "Create" button.

Create a page in Site: Photos by Jane Doe

Name your page:

about

Your page URL: /site/photosbyjanedoe/about change URL

Select a template to use (Learn more)

3- Jane then clicked on the "Layout" menu item and selected a two-column layout.

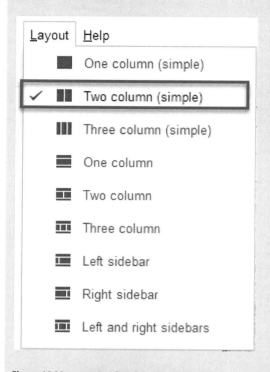

Figure 19 Menu option for changing page layout

4- Jane added a picture of herself on the first column and a short introduction about her works in the right-hand column.

Chapter Six

Videos and Calendars

Two of the most popular items on small business and personal websites are videos and calendars. Videos provide your audience the chance to get a feel for your trade and services using all sensory perceptions except (at the time I am writing this book) the sense of smell. Calendars, on the other hand, allow your website users to keep fully engaged in events that may be of interest to them. The technology that we are going to use for adding videos and calendars, namely, iframes, works the same way. Before you add your video to your site, you first need to upload it into a video-sharing service, such as YouTube or Vimeo.

> Two of the most popular items on small business and personal websites are videos and calendars.

I will show you how you to upload your video to YouTube below. (I am assuming that, at this point, you already have taken a video either with a Smartphone or a camcorder – hopefully not a VHS[5] recorder from the 90's - and have it on your computer as a file).

Working with Videos

How to upload a video to YouTube.

1. Log into YouTube (www.youtube.com) using your Google Account (you can use the user name and password you have used for your Google Sites or Gmail account).
2. Click on "Upload" next to the search bar.

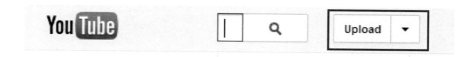

Figure 20 YouTube video upload menu

3. Select your video file from the explorer window, and click on

---

[5] All joking aside, if you have one of video camcorders that take VHS cassettes, you have to first take the cassette to a business that specializes in VHS to DVD conversions and have it converted to a DVD format. Remember, before you take your cassette to the shop, be kind and rewind.

"Upload".

4. Once the video finishes uploading (this might take some time depending on your connection), select the video, and make it public by clicking on "Edit > Info and Setting" and changing the Privacy settings to "Public".

Almost there! You are now ready to embed your video on your Google Sites website. Here are the steps for embedding the video that you just uploaded into YouTube in your website.

Here is how you would embed/add the video you uploaded into your website.

1. Open up YouTube (www.youtube.com), and click on the drop down menu next to the search box. Click on "Video Manager".

The "Video Manager" option allows you to upload videos to YouTube.

Figure 21 YouTube video manager

2. Select your video by clicking on the title.

3. Click on "Share > Embed " link under your video.

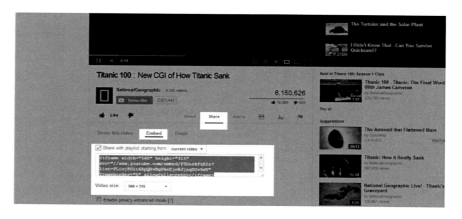

Figure 22 YouTube video embed code

4. Copy the code displayed inside a text box .

(Note that the code for embedding YouTube video starts with the <Iframe> HTML tag. Iframes are used to add content from third-party service providers to a website.)

5. Go back to Google Sites. Select the page where you want to add the video on, and click on the "Edit" icon to edit the page.

6. Once the page editor loads, click on the <HTML> icon to toggle the page contents into HTML code. Clicking on the <HTML> icon is like opening the dashboard of your car and looking at the engine that runs your car. Most likely than not, unless you are one of the "click and clack" brothers[6], you don't need to know about each bolt and nut in your car engine, as long as you can locate the dipstick.

Figure 23 Toggle to HTML

7. Paste the code you got form your YouTube video into the textbox.
8. Click on "Update" to toggle back to the Content View of your page.
9. Click on "Save" to save your page.

Working with Calendars

An online calendar is a good feature to have on your website so that you can keep your online audience engaged in your business activities. Most small businesses and people who don't want to experiment with online calendars resort to adding dates manually. Even though adding events on your website manually adds a personal touch to your web page, it comes with a huge disadvantage. You would have to update your website each time you add a new event or want to remove an old one, wasting valuable time that you could better spend creating value-added items to your business.

A better way of adding a "smart" calendar to your website is to use the Google Calendar widget. It's easy to add a Google Calendar to your site and have it display your engagements with little effort. Here is how to add a Google Calendar to your site.

Let's start first by creating a new calendar.

---

[6] "Click and clack" brothers are hosts of a popular National Public Radio (NPR) program "Car Talk."

Creating a new Google Calendar

1- Log into your Google Sites account.

2- Click on "Calendar" from the top navigation menu.

An online calendar is a good feature to have on your website to keep your online audience engaged.

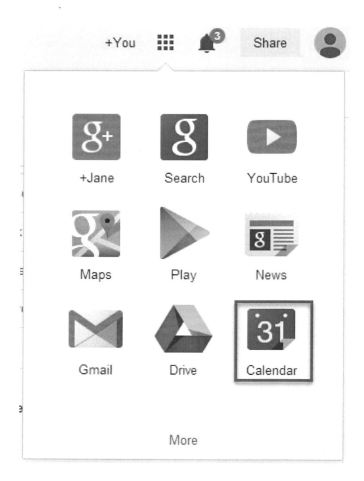

Figure 24 Google Calendar

3- Click on the "Setting" icon, and then click on the text "Settings" from the dropdown menu.

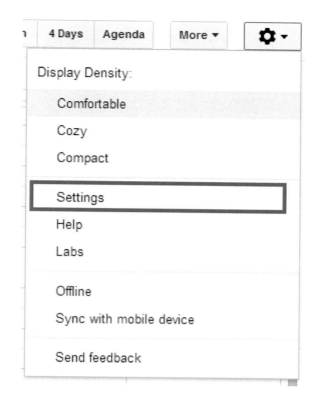

The "Settings" menu shows you all options available to your Google Calendar.

Figure 25 Google Calendar settings

4- Click on the "Calendars" tab.

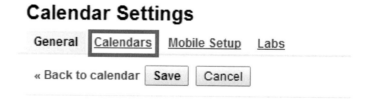

Figure 26 Calendar tab

5- Click on the "Create Calendar" button.

Calendar Settings

General   **Calendars**   Mobile Setup   Labs

« Back to calendar

My Calendars Calendars I can view and modify

Create new calendar   Import calendar   Export calendars

Other Calendars Calendars I can only view

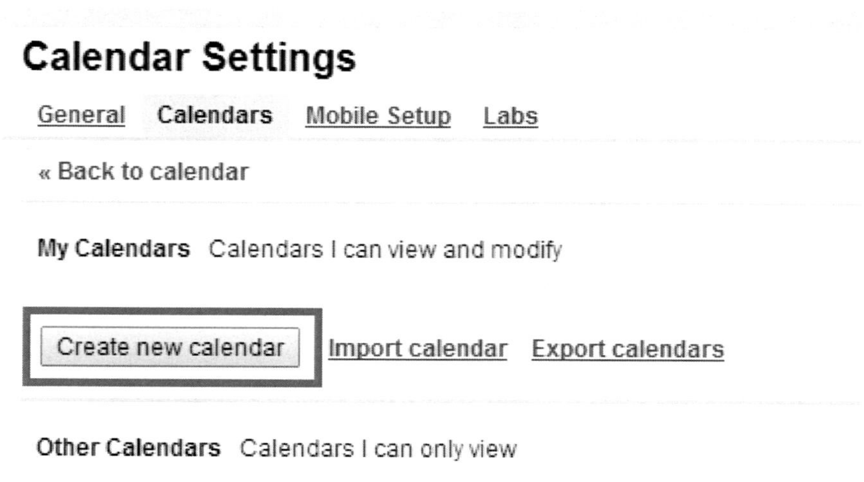

Figure 27 Adding a new calendar.

One Google calendar is assigned to you when you first signed up for any Google Service (e.g. Gmail). I recommend creating a new calendar for your website project to keep things separated between your primary calendar and website calendar.

6- Fill out the name, description, location, and time zone for your calendar.

7- Check on "Make this Calendar Public" check box.

8- Click on "Save".

(Your calendar will now display in the browser.)

9- Click on the "Settings" icon, and then click on the text "Settings" from the dropdown menu.

10- Click on "Calendars" tab.

11- Click on the name of the calendar you just created.

12- Scroll down until you see "Embed this calendar" label.

13- Click on "Customize the color, size, and other options" link.

14- Add a title to your calendar (this will show up on your website, so choose an appropriate title).

15- Change the width and height to "500".

(Ok doubting Thomas … You can customize this later on, but let's go with 500 for now as it works best for your Google site.)

16- Go to the text box under the "Copy and paste the HTML below to include this calendar on your webpage" label, and copy all the code you see in the text box.

You are now ready to add the calendar to your website.

1- Go to your Google Sites page.

44

2- If you already have a page designated for events, select it from the list of pages on your website. If not, just create a new page called "Events".

3- Click on the "Edit Page" icon.

4- Click on the "<HTML>" menu.

Figure 28 Toggle to HTML

The concept of embedding a code (in this case HTML) from one page to another applies to a lot advanced topics in website designing in addition to adding videos and calendars.

5- Paste the code you got from your Google Calendar into your "Events" page.

6- Click on "Update" and then "Save".

Congratulations! You should now see a calendar added into your "Events" page. Depending on how your page looks, you might want to go back and repeat the process with different calendar options.

Case Study – Six

Jane's Webpage Backups

After Jane created all the pages she has in her outline, she wondered what kind of backup options were available in Google Sites. Jane selected one of the pages she created in Chapter four and went over the following menu options to review webpage backup and versioning options.

1- Jane first clicked on the "Settings" icon on a page, and then she clicked on "Revision History".

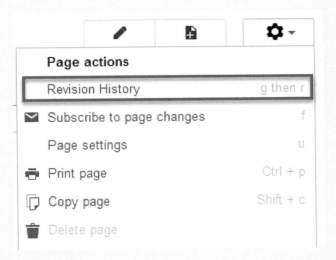

Figure 29 Page revision history

2- Jane noticed that her page already has a "Version 1 (current)" listed on the page history webpage.

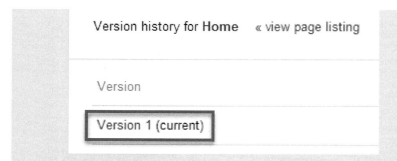

Figure 30 Page versions

Google Sites saves all the changes made to a page in versions. Similar to the steps that Jane took above, you can get to any of the page versions that are available in Google Sites from the "Revision History" menu option in the page settings menu.

If you want to activate a previous version of a page, you simply select the version of the page from the "Revision History" page, and then click on the "Revert to this version" link next to the version number.

Chapter Seven

Working with Forms

If it weren't for forms, the digital world would have been filled with narcissistic dictators who would want to feed you information without anyone's input. If you have narcissistic tendencies, no forms for you! All kidding aside, forms are tools that allow you to actively communicate with your website audience and gather any type of information (including, but not limited to feedback) from your website visitors.

Forms are tools that allow you to actively communicate with your website audience and gather information.

The concept for adding forms to your website is the same as Google Calendar. We will use Google Forms to create a new form where you can collect users' feedback and add it to your website.

Let's get started with creating a new Google form:

1- Log into your Google Sites account.
2- Click on "Drive" from the top navigation menu.
3- Log into Google drive by clicking on the "Drive" menu in your Gmail account view.

Figure 31 Accessing Google Drive

4- Click on "Create" and then "New Form".

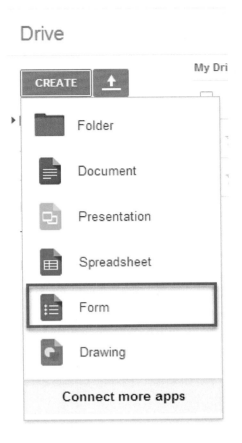

Figure 32 Adding a new Google Form

5- Select the default theme, and select "Ok".

6- Add "Contact Us" on the Question title. (See Figure 22.)

7- Select "paragraph text" for the question type.

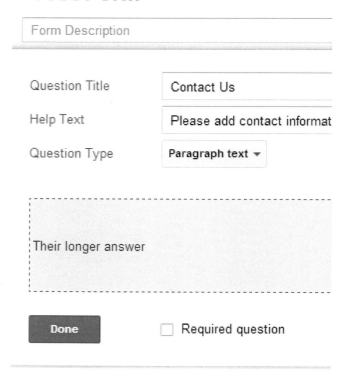

Test Form

Form Description

Question Title	Contact Us
Help Text	Please add contact informat
Question Type	Paragraph text ▾

Their longer answer

Done ☐ Required question

Figure 33 Adding Contact form

8- Select "Done" to save the question. (You can add more questions based on your needs.)

9- **(Here is the good part)** Click on Responses (0) and "Choose response destination" on the top of your newly created form.

Good Part
Choosing a separate destination for the Google form allows you to select how you want to be notified when users fill out the form on your website.

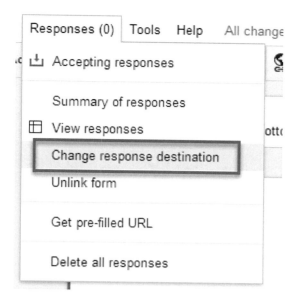

Figure 34 Adding new response destination for a Google form

10- Select all the default values, and click on "Create" to create a spreadsheet to collect all the form responses.

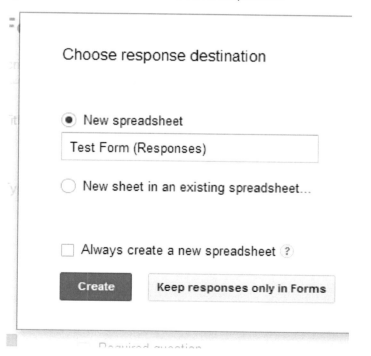

Figure 35 Adding a new spreadsheet to collect form responses

11- You should now see a "View Responses" link on the top of your form.

The "View Responses" option directly links to the spreadsheet that contains a list of responses from your Google form.

12- Click on the "View Responses" link. Once you see the spreadsheet, click on "Tools > Notification" link.

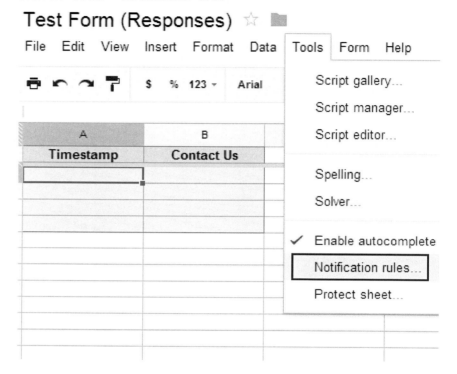

The response collection spreadsheet has a "timestamp." The "timestamp" field contains the date/time that the form was submitted.

Figure 36 Google form responses spreadsheet

13- Select "Any changes are made" and "Email – right away" in the dialog box.

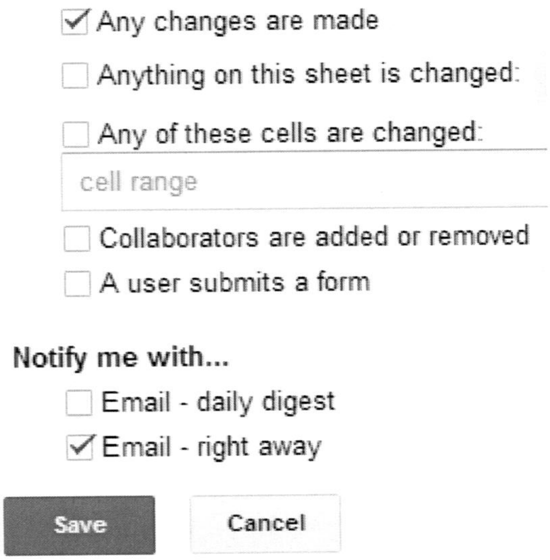

☑ Any changes are made

☐ Anything on this sheet is changed:

☐ Any of these cells are changed:

cell range

☐ Collaborators are added or removed

☐ A user submits a form

Notify me with...

☐ Email - daily digest

☑ Email - right away

[Save]   [Cancel]

The notification option allows you to set how you want to be notified when a form is filled out by an online user.

Figure 37 Setting up email notification

14- Click on "Save" and then "Done" to save the form. (You are now a few clicks away from having a Google form on your site. Have your confetti cannon close by as you will be throwing it at your computer monitor to celebrate the happy union of Google Forms and Google Sites soon)

15- Close your web page, and go back to Google Drive using the "Drive" link from your Gmail account.

16- Click on the form you created in **step 4**.

17- Once the form loads, click on "File > Embed".

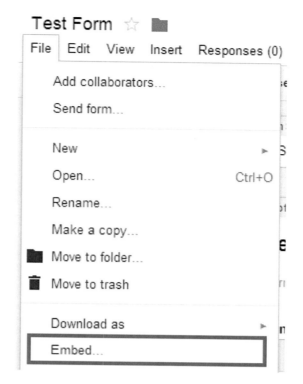

Once a Google form is created in "Google Drives," you can add it to your website by using the "Embed..." option.

Figure 38 Embedding a Google form

Embed form

Paste HTML to embed in website

<iframe src="https://docs.google.com/forms/d/1-LFh_Om

Custom size

Press Ctrl+C to copy.

Width (in pixels) 760   Height (in pixels) 500

Done

Figure 39 HTML code for embedding a Google form

You now have the HTML code that you can add to your Google site to embed your form. Here is how you add the form to your Google site:

1- Go to your Google Sites account.
2- If you already have a page designated for a form, select it from the list of pages on your website. If not, just create a new page.

3- Click on "Edit Page" icon.

4- Once the page editor loads, click on the "<HTML>" icon.

5- Paste the code you got from your Google form into the page you selected or created.

6- Click on "Update" then "Save".

If you successfully completed the activity, congratulations! You now have a form on your website. Don't be afraid to use the confetti. If you feel like a little shout and dance interlude is appropriate, go for it. I am sure you can do better than the internet sensation dancing cockatoo.

Case Study – Seven

Jane shrunk her site

Jane wanted her home page (the tile of images) and detail pages to be center-aligned. With her knowledge of photography, Jane knows that sometimes a smaller canvas results in a more vibrant photo. To test the theory, Jane used the following steps to shrink the website width by 40%.

1- Jane clicked on the "Settings" icon on her home page option and then selected the "Edit site layout"

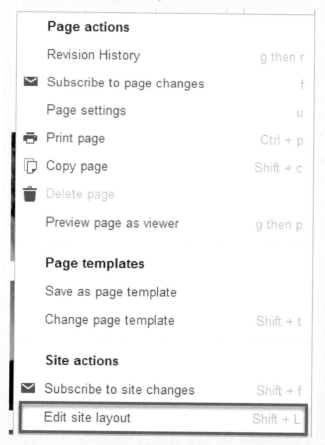

Figure 40 Site layout menu option

2- Jane changed the "Site Width" to the "Custom" option and added

"60%" in the width field.

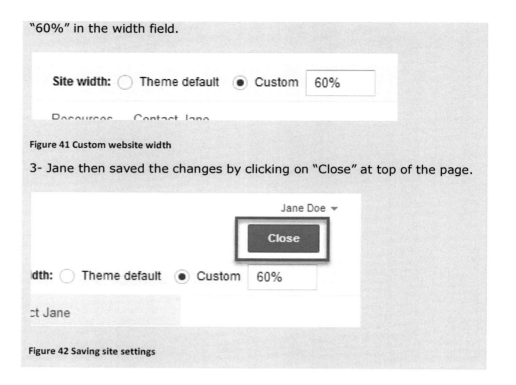

Figure 41 Custom website width

3- Jane then saved the changes by clicking on "Close" at top of the page.

Figure 42 Saving site settings

Chapter Eight

Customizing Your Site

If you finished all the activities in the previous Chapters, you now should have your a website set up with text, images, a calendar of events, and a form. Your website might look plain as we were using the basic template for the Google site so far. In this Chapter, though, we're going to spice things up by customizing the general look and feel or your website.

Let's get started.

Working With Themes

Google Sites has a number of themes you can use to make your site visually appealing.

Google sites has a number of themes you can use to make your site visually appealing. Here are the steps to swap the basic template that we are using with another theme.

1- Go to your Google Sites account.
2- Click on "More > Manage Site".
3- Click on "Themes, Colors and Fonts".
4- Click of the "Base Theme" dropdown.

Figure 43 Browsing for Base Themes

5- Choose the theme that fits your needs, and click on "select" to preview the theme.
6- If you like the changes, click on "Save" to apply the theme to your website.

Even though the design and theme you select varies with your personal preference and your website content, here are few interesting base templates to you might want to explore.

Conservative themes (Good for a portfolio website)

- All "Solitude" based templates (e.g. Solitude: Navy, Solitude: Cherry, Solitude: Spice)

- Micro Blueprint

Things and places (Good for small businesses)

- All "Tera" based themes (e.g. Tera:Water, Tera:Ice, Tera:Ruby)

Customizing Text

Text is one of the most important components of your website. The type, color, and size of font sets the tone for your entire website.

To make your website look professional and polished, avoid using the following:

- All CAPS (Uppercase alphabets for words – unless you are referring to acronyms)

- Fonts that are too big (more than 18pts) and

- Fonts that are too small (less than 10pts)

Here are the steps to make the text on your website have a consistent font size.

1. Bring up the page editor by clicking on the "Edit" icon on your website page.

2. Highlight all text in the text editor.

3. Click on the "Remove Formatting" icon.

The "Remove Formatting" option cleans up your text and makes the font-size consistent on your web page.

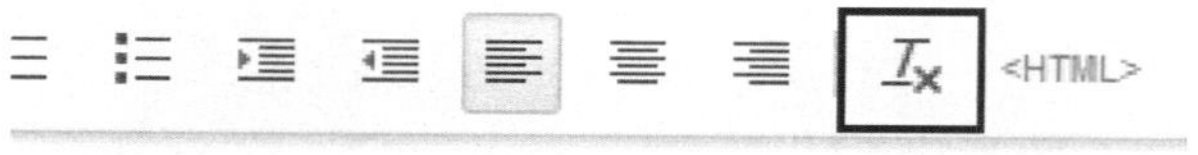

Figure 44 Removing text formatting

All your web page text will now have a consistent font-size that is easy to read for your website visitors. If you have a title for your website content –

highlight the title, and select a font size of "16pts" or "18pts". Making the title bold also improves the look and feel of the web page.

Lorem Ipsum

Figure 45 Bold 16pts font Page Title

Customizing Images

Even though adding an image to a web page is easy (if you followed the instructions provided in previous Chapters), it is somewhat challenging to format an image's size without looking at a web page's HTML code. Here are some formatting tips that will help you customize images on your website.

The first customization that you can do with an image is adjusting its size.

1. To adjust an image size, you first click on the "Edit" icon to edit a page and activate the page editor.

2. Once the page editor loads, select the image by clicking on it.

3. The image editor loads up, and you can select "S", "M", or "L" to make the image small, medium, or large.

The image editor gives you an option to align and resize images.

Figure 46 Adjusting image size

In some instances, the image size "S", "M", and "L" might not exactly give you the image size you want on your web page. You have to look at the web page HTML code if you want to use a custom image size.

Here are the steps for creating custom image sizes on a web page.

1. First make sure you are using the "Original" image size for your image.

Figure 47 Original image size

2. Scroll up to the top of your page editor, and click on <HTML> toggle
    button.

Figure 48 HTML toggle

3. Locate the "<img .." tag in the HTML code.

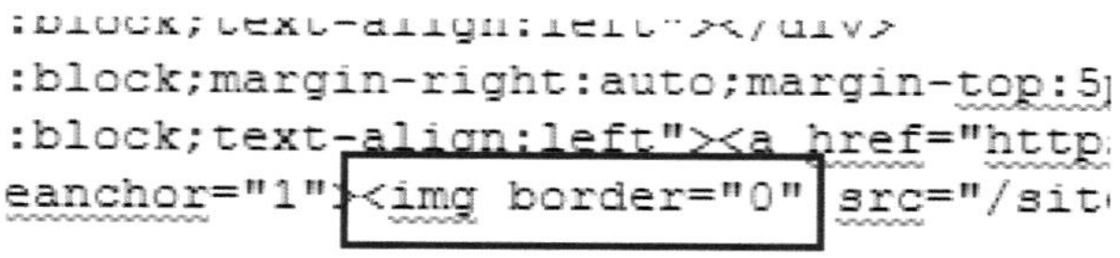

```
:block;text-align:left"></div>
:block;margin-right:auto;margin-top:5]
:block;text-align:left"><a href="http
eanchor="1"><img border="0" src="/sit
```

Figure 49 Image (img) tag

4. Add "Width=Your image size" to the code inside the "<img .." tag. For
    example, if you want your image to have a 400px size, add "width=400"
    in the image tag (see picture below).

Note that there is
space before and after
"width=400".

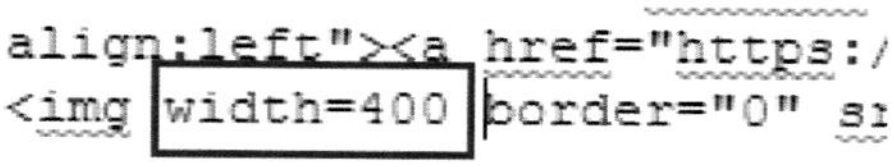

```
align:left"><a href="https:/
<img width=400 border="0" s:
```

Figure 50 Custom image size

You can also make the image align on left, center, or right by
selecting the image alignment menus.

Figure 51 Aligning image

Another attractive enhancement for images in your web page is to align an image to the left and have text wrap around it. This is especially an attractive enhancement to your web page if you have multiple small images you want to add.

To align your image to the left, select the image by clicking on it, and use the "Wrap On" menu option on the image editor.

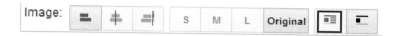

Figure 52 Wrap On menu item

Customizing iframes

iframes (<iframe src=""></iframe>) are used to embed features such as videos, calendars, and forms to your website. In Chapter six, we went over how to add video and calendars to your web using iframes, and in Chapter seven, we saw how iframes are used to add a form into a web page.

Even though the process of adding code that contains iframes from online services such as YouTube, Google Calendar, and Google Forms is straightforward, there might be instances where you want to adjust the width and height of a YouTube video, a Google calendar, or a Google form before or after adding it to your web page.

Here are the steps for adjusting the height and width of an iframe that you got from a third-party online service (e.g. YouTube, Google Calendar, Google Forms):

1. Go to the service provider's website, and get the HTML code to embed in your website.
   (In this example, I am going to use YouTube.)

Iframes are used to add third-party tools, such as videos, forms, and calendars to a web page.

2. Locate the width and height block in the HTML code.

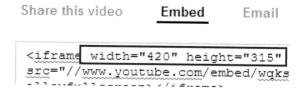

Figure 53 Updating height and width of an iframe

3. Update the width and height as needed.

4. In some instances, you might also want to add the following code (frameborder="0") to your iframe HTML code so that the iframe does not show any borders. (Some service providers, such as YouTube, automatically add the zero border code for you .)

Note that there is a space before and after "frameborder=0".

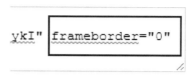

Figure 54 Removing a border from an iframe

Working With Tables

A table is also a good feature to add to your website, especially if you have a list of items to display. Here is how to add a table into a web page.

1. Turn the page editor on by clicking on the "Edit" button at the top of your Google Sites web page.

2. Click on "Table > Insert Table" from the top navigation menu on the page editor.

I recommend adding tables only if you have a list of more than three items to display on a web page.

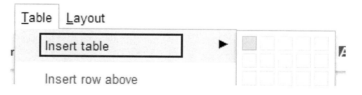

Figure 55 Inserting a table

3. Select the number of rows and columns you want for the table. (In the example below, the new table will have three columns and two rows.)

Figure 56 Adding columns and rows (three columns and two rows)

4. Highlight the number of columns and rows you want for your table by dragging your mouse over the square boxes that show up next to the "Inset table" menu item. If you want a table with two rows and three columns, highlight two rows and three columns on the table insert menu (see figure 57) using you mouse and the table with corresponding rows and columns will be added to your webpage after you highlight your row and column selection and click on the panel.

    By default, all tables added via the page editor come with borders. You can turn the table borders off by using the following steps:

1. First add a table to your web page, and add all the text and image you want to display inside the table cells.
    (It's important to add the table contents first because it will be very difficult to locate the column/row lines once the table borders are turned off.)

2. Click on <HTML> on the page editor to view the web page's code

3. Locate the border and width segment of your table in the <table> HTML tag.

```
<table border="1"
width: 1px;">
```

Figure 57 Adjusting table border

4. Change the (border="1") to (border="0") and the(width: 1px) to (width: 0px).

5. Click on "Update" to toggle back to the page view mode. Your table will now have no borders.

How to get a domain name to go with your site

In addition to accessing your site via the very long Google Sites link (https://sites.google.com/site/[YourSite]), you can also get your own domain name for your website. There are many domain name registrars that sell domain names, such as namecheap.com and domain.com, to buy a domain name.

It's difficult to give you a definitive set of instructions on how to associate your domain name with your Google site as each domain registrar uses its own web interface to manage your domain name. However, I will give you some general ideas on how to associate your domain name with your site.

How to associate your Google site with a custom domain name

The first step for associating your Google site with a custom domain name (for example photosbyjanedoe.com) to purchasing a domain name. Domain names can be purchased from domain name registrars such as NameCheap.com and Domain.com.

To give you some ideas on domain name purchasing process, I have outlined the steps for purchasing a new site from one of the domain name registrars, namely NameCheap.com, below.

1- Go to the link "http://www.namecheap.com/?aff=72834"

Figure 58 Namecheap website

2- Type in the domain name you want for your website in the search box

3- If the domain name is available you will see the message "This domain name is available!" with a shopping cart option to buy the domain name

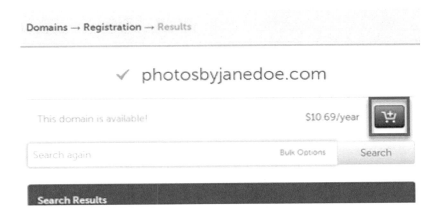

Figure 59 Domain name shopping cart

4- Once you add the domain name to the shopping cart you can then finalize the domain name purchase by entering your payment information

4- After you purchased your domain name. You can go to the "Manage Domains" option to view your domain name.

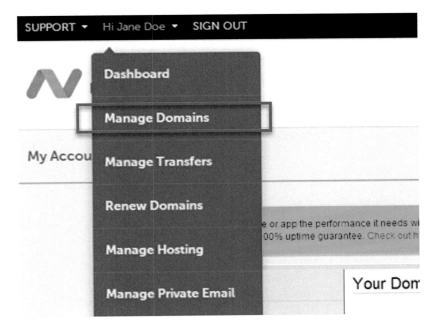

Figure 60 Namecheap manage domains option

I assume at this point you already have bought a domain name and are somewhat familiar with logging into your domain registrar's website. Here are the steps for associating your domain name to your Google Sites hosted website.

1- First head to the Google Webmaster Tool website by going to the following link: www.google.com/webmasters/
(The account you have used for Google Sites will work for the Google Webmaster service.)
2- Follow the instructions on the screen to verify your domain ownership.
(The process usually involves uploading a test file – which is provided to you by the Google Webmaster Tool website –or making few updates on your Domain registrar's website.)

Here is how you associate your domain name with Google Sites:

1- Go to your Google Sites account.
2- Click on "More > Manage Site".
3- Click on "Web Address".
4- Add your domain name in the "Add Web Address" box.

Almost there! Now we need to go back to your domain registrar's account, and you will make some changes to your domain settings so that your domain registrar knows where to send internet traffic coming to your website.

CNAMEs are like car license plates for domain name controllers. CNAMES display to internet traffic where a particular website is located.

1- Go to your domain registrar's website.
2- Look for an option called "CNAME" (you will usually find the option in a user interface that shows you your domain bindings).

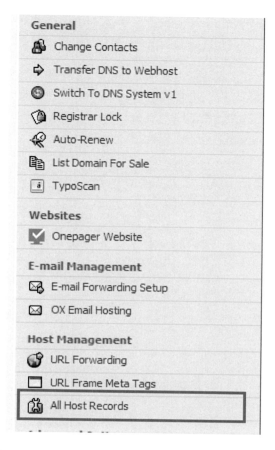

General
- Change Contacts
- Transfer DNS to Webhost
- Switch To DNS System v1
- Registrar Lock
- Auto-Renew
- List Domain For Sale
- TypoScan

Websites
- Onepager Website

E-mail Management
- E-mail Forwarding Setup
- OX Email Hosting

Host Management
- URL Forwarding
- URL Frame Meta Tags
- All Host Records

Figure 61 "All Host Records" option for NameCheap

3- When you get to the screen, see if there is an entry that has "WWW" in the list of "CNAME" options.

4- If you find the "WWW", delete the entry.

5- Click on the option to add a new CNAME.

6- Put in the following values in the field:

Name = "WWW"

IP Address/URL = ghs.google.com

Modify Domain: photosbyjanedoe.com

HOST NAME	IP ADDRESS/ URL	RECORD TYPE
@	http://www.photosbyjan	URL Redirect
www	ghs.google.com.	CNAME (Alias)

Figure 62 CNAME record in NameCheap.com for custom domain name

As the websites of domain registrars are always evolving you need to spend some time to research and understand the their service offering before making an online purchase.

That's it! You are now a proud owner of a website in Google Sites that maps to your own domain name. Note - it might take anywhere between 20 minutes to 24 hours for the domain name to be rerouted to your Google site with your new custom domain name.

Case Study – Eight

Jane launches her new portfolio website

Jane's Home page updates

When Jane created the home page of her new website, she noticed a black border around each image on the home page. From the lessons in Chapter Two, Jane has learned that she can edit some of the code that is generated by Google Sites by clicking on the HTML editor on a page and adding or removing certain characters.

Here is what Jane's home page looked like before applying updates and removing borders around the images.

Home   About Jane   Projects   Calendar   Resources   Contact

Home

Figure 63 Jane's home page before updates

Jane turned off the black border around images on the home page using the following steps:

1- Jane clicked on the edit icon on her home page.

2- Once in edit mode, Jane clicked on the "HTML" menu item to see what is under the hood of her home page.

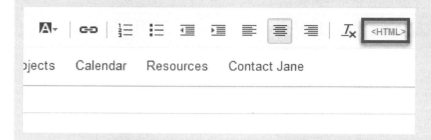

Figure 64 HTML editor

3- Jane then removed the highlighted code (below) that is automatically generated by Google Sites by **border="0"**.

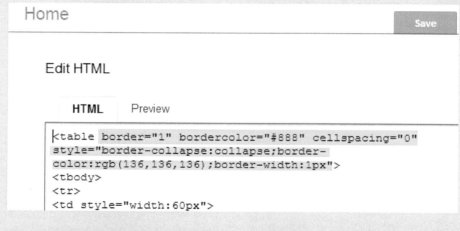

Figure 65 HTML code before Jane updated her home page

Figure 66 HTML code of Jane's home page after the update

4- Jane then clicked "Save" to save her change.

Jane's Amazon© Storefront

Jane wanted a feature to integrate the new Amazon© aStore™ she created in Chapter two with the new website. She has already created an Amazon© aStore™ following the steps outlined in Chapter Two and additional instructions provided by Amazon.

Jane used the following steps to add the Amazon© aStore™ to her new Google site:

1- Jane went to the Amazon© aStore™ she created and located the "Sidebar Widget" code for her new storefront .

Figure 67 Steps for creating widgets in Amazon© aStore™

The "Sidebar Widget" code is located in step 4 (Get Link) of creating/customizing an Amazon© aStore™.

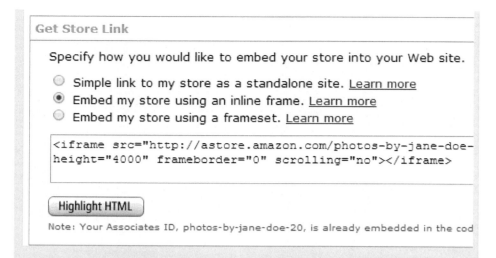

Figure 68 Embed code for Amazon© aStore™

2- Jane copied the code she got from Amazon.

3- Jane pasted the code into her "Resources" page by first clicking on the "HTML" menu item in the text editor.

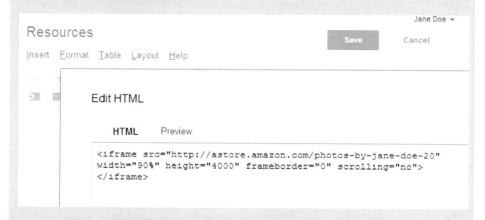

Figure 69 Adding Amazon© aStore™ embed code on Google Sites page

Domain Name for Jane's New Website

Jane wanted her audience to access her website easily on the web, so she explored options to have her own domain name for the site. Fortunately, the website address "www.photosbyjanedoe.com" was available, so she went ahead and paid registration fees (at the time this book is written) $10.69 for one full-year subscription.

Jane followed the steps to associate the new domain name she bought from her domain registrar with her new Google site.

1- Jane first registered her new domain name on Google Webmasters tools (https://www.google.com/webmasters/) following instructions on the website.

2- After verifying the domain name on the Google Webmasters website, Jane then went to her Google site and clicked on the settings icon. Then she selected the "Manage site" option

3- In the "Web Address" field, she typed in www.photosbyjanedoe.com, and clicked on the "Add" button.

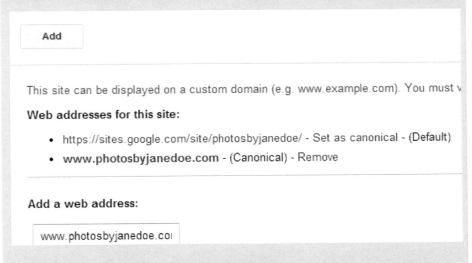

Figure 70 Adding new website domain name in Google Sites

4- Jane then went to her domain registrar's website and added the following "CNAME" records:

"www" and "ghs.google.com"

Figure 71 Modifying website CNAME

Tracking Website Visitors

Jane wanted to track her website visitors to see the most popular pages on her site. Jane has heard that Google Analytics, another product from Google, allows a website to track website visitors. Jane used the following steps to sign up for a Google Analytics account and start tracking her website visitors.

1- Jane went to the Google Analytics website (http://www.google.com/analytics).

2- Jane clicked on "Sign Up" to sign up for the service.

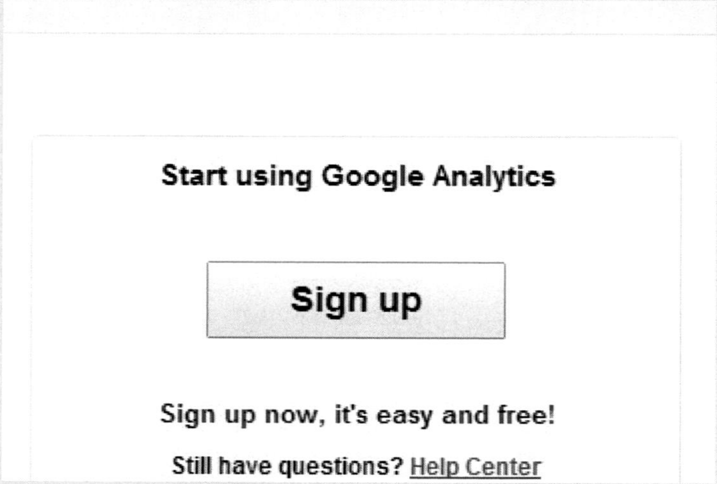

Start using Google Analytics

Sign up

Sign up now, it's easy and free!

Still have questions? Help Center

Figure 72 Signing up for Google Analytics

3- Jane filled out the details of her website.

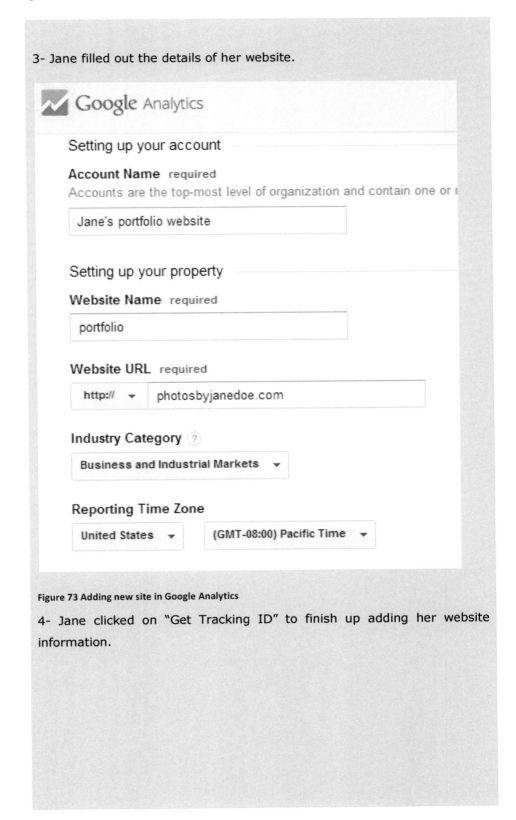

Figure 73 Adding new site in Google Analytics

4- Jane clicked on "Get Tracking ID" to finish up adding her website information.

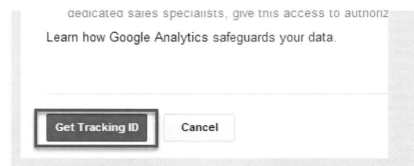

Learn how Google Analytics safeguards your data.

Get Tracking ID   Cancel

Figure 74 Tracking ID for Google Analytics

5- Jane then clicked on the "Property Settings" to locate the tracking ID for her new website.

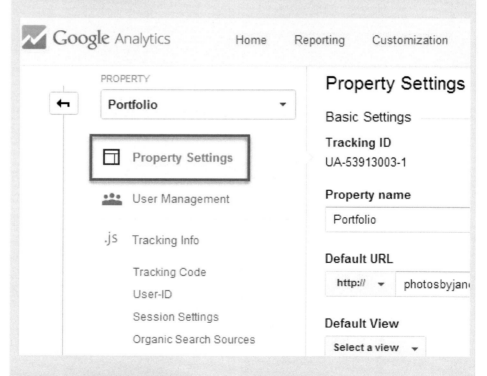

Figure 75 Google Analytics site settings

6- Jane copied the tracking code and went to her Google site.

7- Jane clicked on her website setting in Google Sites and clicked on "Mange Site".

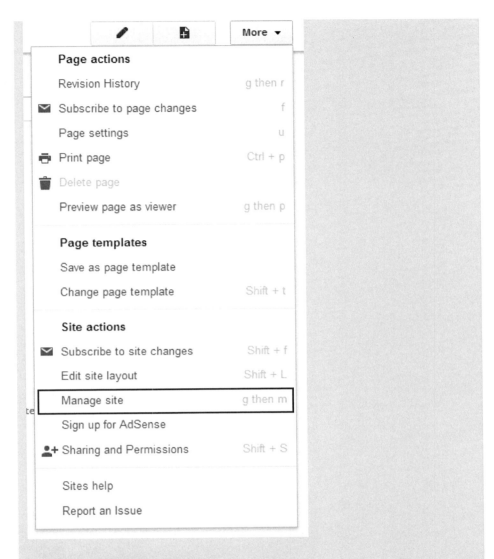

Figure 76 Manage site menu in Google Sites

Figure 77 Google Sites website management menu option

8- Jane scrolled down to the "Statistics" section of her website properties and turned visitor tracking on by selecting the "Use Google Analytics" option from the dropdown menu.

9- Jane then pasted the code she got from Google Analytics into the "Analytics Web Property" field.

Figure 78 Google Analytics web property ID

10 - Jane then clicked "Save" to complete adding tracking code to her new website.

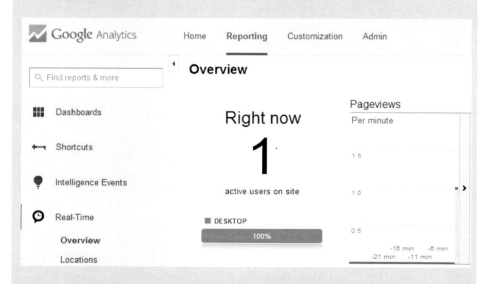

Figure 79 Real-time website analytics on Jane's new website

After saving the website settings, Jane was able to track visitors to her website using Google Analytics.

Google Analytics is a member of a slew of services that provide optimization tools for website to keep web pages running like well-oiled-machine. I will spare you the details for now and perhaps revisit the topic in another similar publication.